Life Cycles

Frog

Louise Spilsbury

Heinemann Library
Chicago, Illinois

Customer Service   888-454-2279

Visit our website at www.heinemannlibrary.com

Photo research by Maria Joannou and Debra Weatherley
Designed by Michelle Lisseter
Printed and bound in China by South China Printing Company

09 08 07 06 05
10 9 8 7 6 5 4 3 2 1

Library of Congress Cataloging-in-Publication Data
Spilsbury, Louise.
  Frog / Louise Spilsbury.
       p. cm. -- (Life cycles)
  Includes index.
  ISBN 1-4034-6772-2 (hard cover) -- ISBN 1-4034-6777-3 (paper back)
  1. Frogs--Life cycles--Juvenile literature. I. Title. II. Series.
  QL668.E2S7385 2005
  597.8'9--dc22

                                        2004020860

Acknowledgments
The author and publisher are grateful to the following for permission to reproduce copyright material: Ardea p
(Ian Beames), 10 (John Mason); Bruce Coleman pp. 16 (Jane Burton), 17 (Kim Taylor), 20 (M.P.L. Fogden), 23
(webbed feet, M.P.L. Fogden); Ecoscene (Anthony Cooper) pp. 6, 23 (female, lay); FLPA pp. 4 (C. Newton), 5 (Ma
B. Withers), 9 (Foto Natura Stock), 18 (Jurgen & Christine Sohns), 23 (hatch, Foto Natura Stock); Getty Images p
(Stone); Nature Picture Library p. 19 (Nick Garbutt); NHPA p. 8 (Stephen Dalton); Oxford Scientific Films pp. 12,
23 (insects, Robert Parks); Papilio pp. 14 (Robert Pickett), 15 (Robert Pickett), 22 (Clive Druett), back cover (webb
feet, Clive Druett); Science Photo Library (Gusto) pp. 11, back cover (tadpoles)

Cover photograph of a frog reproduced with permission of Ardea (John Daniels)

Every effort has been made to contact copyright holders of any material reproduced in this book. Any omission
will be rectified in subsequent printings if notice is given to the publisher.

Many thanks to the teachers, library media specialists, reading instructors, and educational consultants who have
helped develop the Read and Learn/Lee y aprende brand.

Contents

Some words are shown in bold, **like this.** You can find the in the picture glossary on page 23.

What Is a Frog?

This is a frog.

Frogs are small animals that can live on land and in water.

Frogs start life underwater.

A frog also starts life inside an egg.

Where Do Frogs Lay Eggs?

Female frogs **lay** eggs in water.

They lay hundreds of eggs
at a time.

The eggs are covered in a kind of jelly.

The jelly protects the babies inside the eggs.

What Do Frogs' Eggs Look Like?

These are a frog's eggs.

They are round and very small.

The black shape inside each egg will grow into a young frog.

Tadpoles **hatch** out of the eggs.

What Are Tadpoles?

Tadpoles are young frogs.

Each tadpole has a long tail.

Tadpoles use their tails to swim.

Soon, the tadpoles will grow legs.

When Do Tadpoles Grow Legs?

When the tadpole is 8 weeks old it grows back legs.

Its body is long.

The tadpoles use their legs to swim faster.

When Do Tadpoles Become Frogs?

At 9 weeks old, the tadpole grows front legs.

The frog has four **webbed feet.**

Then, the tail gets much smaller.

Now it looks more like a
little frog.

What Do Frogs Eat?

Frogs eat flies and other **insects.**

They eat worms, too.

Frogs jump to catch insects.

Their long back legs help them jump high.

How Do Frogs Stay Safe?

Some animals like to eat frogs.

Frogs jump away from danger.

Frogs also come out at night.

It is harder for other animals to catch them at night.

Where Do Frogs Live?

Frogs live in damp places on land.

They also live near plants.

They live near ponds too.

They go back into water to lay eggs of their own.

Frog Diagram

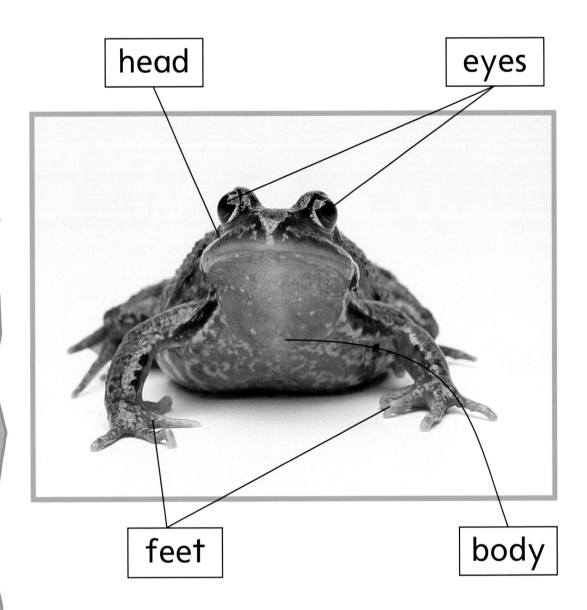

head

eyes

feet

body

Picture Glossary

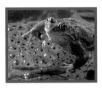

female
page 6
girl animal that lays eggs or has babies

hatch
page 9
come out of an egg

insect
pages 16, 17
animal with six legs and usually two pairs of wings

lay
page 6
when an egg comes out of an animal's body

webbed feet
page 14
animal feet that have skin between the toes

Note to Parents and Teachers

Reading for information is an important part of a child's literacy development. Learning begins with a question about something. Help children think of themselves as investigators and researchers by encouraging their questions about the world around them. Each chapter in this book begins with a question. Read the question together. Look at the pictures. Talk about what you think the answer might be. Then read the text to find out if your predictions were correct. Think of other questions you could ask about the topic, and discuss where you might find the answers. Assist children in using the picture glossary and the index to practice new vocabulary and research skills.

Index